W9-AAW-135

Demeter

BY VIRGINIA LOH-HAGAN

Gods and goddesses were the main characters of myths. Myths are traditional stories from ancient cultures. Storytellers answered questions about the world by creating exciting explanations. People thought myths were true. Myths explained the unexplainable. They helped people make sense of human behavior and nature. Today, we use science to explain the world. But people still love myths. Myths may not be literally true. But they have meaning. They tell us something about our history and culture.

45th Parallel Press

Published in the United States of America by Cherry Lake Publishing
Ann Arbor, Michigan
www.cherrylakepublishing.com

Content Adviser: Matthew Wellenbach, Catholic Memorial School, West Roxbury, MA
Reading Adviser: Marla Conn MS, Ed., Literacy specialist, Read-Ability, Inc.
Book Designer: Jen Wahi

Photo Credits: © Pidgorna Ievgeniia/Shutterstock.com, 5; © Nomad_Soul/Shutterstock.com, 6; © Nadya Korobkova/Shutterstock.com, 8; © symbiot/Shutterstock.com, 11; © manifeesto/istockphoto.com, 13; © Vuk Kostic/Shutterstock.com, 15; © Elena Schweitzer/Shutterstock.com, 18; Howard David Johnson, 2016, 19; © Dance60/Dreamstime.com, 21; © Sylphe_7/istockphoto.com, 22; © valentinrussanov/istockphoto.com, 25; © North Wind Picture Archives/Alamy Stock Photo, 27; © Chronicle/Alamy Stock Photo, 29; © Howard David Johnson, 2016, Cover; various art elements throughout, shutterstock.com

45th Parallel Press is an imprint of Cherry Lake Publishing.

Library of Congress Cataloging-in-Publication Data

Names: Loh-Hagan, Virginia, author.
Title: Demeter / by Virginia Loh-Hagan.
Description: Ann Arbor : Cherry Lake Publishing, [2017] | Series: Gods and
    goddesses of the ancient world | Includes bibliographical references and
    index.
Identifiers: LCCN 2016031220| ISBN 9781634721387 (hardcover) | ISBN
    9781634722704 (pbk.) | ISBN 9781634722049 (pdf) | ISBN 9781634723367
    (ebook)
Subjects: LCSH: Demeter (Greek deity)--Juvenile literature. | Goddesses,
    Greek--Juvenile literature. | Mythology, Greek--Juvenile literature.
Classification: LCC BL820.C5 L64 2017 | DDC 292.2/114--dc23
LC record available at https://lccn.loc.gov/2016031220

Printed in the United States of America
Corporate Graphics

ABOUT THE AUTHOR:

Dr. Virginia Loh-Hagan is an author, university professor, former classroom teacher, and curriculum designer. She appreciates the harvests brought by Demeter. Eating is her favorite hobby. She lives in San Diego with her very tall husband and very naughty dogs. To learn more about her, visit www.virginialoh.com.

TABLE OF CONTENTS

CHAPTER 1

AN INDEPENDENT WOMAN

Who is Demeter? How was she born? What did she look like?

Demeter was a Greek goddess. She was one of the 12 **Olympians**. These gods ruled over all of the gods. They lived on Mount Olympus. Mount Olympus is in Greece. It's the highest mountain in Greece.

Demeter's parents were Cronus and Rhea. They were **Titans**. Titans were giant gods. They ruled until the Olympians took over.

Cronus was told that a son would take away his power.

So, Cronus ate his children. Demeter was one of them. Rhea saved one child, Zeus. Later, Zeus came back. He tricked Cronus. He poisoned him. Cronus threw up Demeter and the others.

Demeter was important. Gods and mortals respected her.

Demeter liked being outdoors.

Zeus led a war against the Titans. Demeter and her **siblings** won. Siblings mean brothers and sisters.

Demeter was different from her siblings. She preferred to roam the earth. She lived in open fields. She preferred to be with her **mortal** worshippers. Mortal means human. She lived in her temples. She rarely went to Mount Olympus.

Demeter was important to mortals. She was the goddess of harvest. She was in charge of grains. She was in charge of farming. She was in charge of **fertility**. Fertility means growth and bounty.

Family Tree

Grandparents: Uranus (Father Sky) and Gaia (Mother Earth)

Parents: Cronus (god of time) and Rhea (goddess of fertility)

Brothers: Zeus (god of the sky), Hades (god of the underworld), Poseidon (god of the seas)

Sisters: Hera (goddess of women and marriage), Hestia (goddess of the hearth and family)

Spouse: No husband, several lovers

Children: Persephone (Queen of the Underworld), Despoina (goddess of mysteries), Arion (immortal horse), Plutus (god of wealth), Philomelus (inventor of the wagon)

Demeter was beautiful. She had golden hair. It looked like grain. Demeter braided her hair. Braids show a connection to nature. Her braids looked like dried wheat. She had large brown eyes. She wore a golden dress. The dress was the color of a wheat harvest.

Demeter chose not to marry. She didn't have a husband. But she had several lovers. She had several children. Her children had different fathers. Her favorite child was Persephone. Zeus was Persephone's father.

Demeter was an independent woman. She did whatever she wanted. She didn't need men to make her powerful. She had her own powers.

 Demeter braided her hair with dried grass and flowers.

CHAPTER 2

GOOD GROWING

What are Demeter's powers? What did she contribute to mankind?

Demeter provided the world's food source. She made crops grow. She commanded the seasons. She protected the land. She controlled the laws of nature. She controlled life and death.

Demeter changed into an old woman. She asked King Celeus and Queen Metanira for help. They helped her. Demeter nursed their sons. The sons were named Demophon and Triptolemus. She rewarded the king and queen's kindness. She tried to make Demophon **immortal**. Immortal means living forever. She put Demophon in a fire. She wanted to burn away his mortal parts. Metanira screamed. So, Demeter stopped. Instead, she taught Triptolemus how to farm. Triptolemus taught other people.

Demeter had many powers. She changed things into plants. She made plants do whatever she wanted. She controlled weather. She controlled anything made from earth.

The first loaf of bread made from the yearly harvest was given to Demeter.

All in the Family

Demeter was pursued by Poseidon. Poseidon was her brother. She disguised herself as a horse. She hid. Poseidon pretended to be a horse. He mated with Demeter. They had twins. The twins were named Arion and Despoina. Arion was immortal. Arion looked like a horse. But he had wings. He also had human feet. He was fast. No one in a chariot race could pass him. He used his wings to speed up. Sometimes, he pulled Poseidon's chariot. Arion could speak and was very smart. Despoina was Arion's twin sister. She was the goddess of mysteries of Arcadian cults. Only worshippers could say her name. Like her mother, she was celebrated for bringing fertility.

Demeter worked with other goddesses to help pregnant women and babies.

She gave gifts to people. She created nature. Phytalos welcomed Demeter into his home. He was kind. Demeter rewarded him. She gave him the first fig tree.

Demeter helped create life. She helped women get pregnant. She worked with other goddesses. Artemis helped pregnant women. Eileithyia helped with childbirth. Hera helped mothers care for their babies. Demeter cared about life.

CHAPTER 3

TURNING COLD

Who are some of Demeter's lovers? How and why did she punish others?

Demeter wasn't lucky in love.

Zeus tricked Demeter. He changed into a bull. They had Persephone. Poseidon tricked Demeter. He changed into a horse. They had twins. Demeter loved her children. But she felt betrayed. She was angry at her brothers. She pushed her anger into a river. The river was called Ladon.

Demeter loved a mortal. His name was Iasion. They met at a wedding. All the gods were there. Demeter and Iasion fell in love. This made Zeus mad. He didn't like goddesses hanging out with mortals. He reacted badly. He killed Iasion with a thunderbolt. Demeter turned Iasion into a **constellation**. Constellations are star patterns.

Demeter was very protective. She harmed those who offended her. She got even.

She punished Ascalaphus. Ascalaphus helped Hades. Hades kidnapped Demeter's daughter. This made Demeter mad.

Demeter was powerful, but her brothers were more powerful.

Real World Connection

Like Demeter, Tiffany Segee grows things. She worked with her family to grow a garden. Her husband is Vernon. Her daughters are Jai'Neil, Dee'Anna, and Jai'Lynn. The Segee family lives in Los Angeles. They grew a 28-pound (12.7 kilograms) organic cucumber. They tried to get a world record. A neighbor gave them an albino cucumber plant. The family planted it. They didn't use fertilizer. They just used water. They hung its vine on a gate. They watched it grow. Segee said, "We shared it with people. There was just too much for us to eat." Segee is happy that her daughters are now interested in gardening.

Owls were sacred to Demeter and Athena.

She buried Ascalaphus under a rock. She trapped him in the underworld. Ascalaphus was rescued. Demeter refused to let him go. She sprinkled him with magic river water. She turned him into a screech owl.

Demeter punished Erysichthon. Erysichthon cut down Demeter's trees. He built a dining hall. Demeter cursed him. She made him be hungry forever. Erysichthon ended up eating himself.

Demeter punished Kolontas. She asked him for shelter. He refused. He was rude to her. She burned down his house. She burned him alive.

She punished Minthe. Minthe said she was prettier than Demeter's daughter, Persephone. Demeter turned Minthe into a mint plant.

She punished Lynkos. Lynkos was a king. He tried to kill Triptolemus. Triptolemus served Demeter. Demeter turned Lynkos into a lynx.

She punished Askalabos. Askalabos made fun of Demeter. Demeter turned him into a lizard.

She punished some **maidens**. Maidens are young, pretty women. Demeter wanted their help. The maidens said no. Demeter turned them into **Sirens**. Sirens were monsters. They were half-women. They were half-birds.

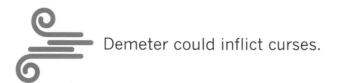 Demeter could inflict curses.

CHAPTER 4

DRAGONS AND MORE!

What are Demeter's symbols? What do her dragons do?

Demeter had many symbols. She carried **sheaves** of wheat. Sheaves are bundles. She had a **cornucopia**. This is a container. It's shaped like a goat's horn. It held grains and breads. Demeter liked pigs. She was the goddess of pig farming. Mortals gave her pigs' blood. They thought it made the land more fertile.

Demeter had many weapons. She had a long, golden sword. She was called the Lady of the Golden Blade. She carried a torch. The torch helped her find her kidnapped daughter.

Demeter had dragons. Her dragons had wings. They were called Demeter's Dragons. Demeter used her dragons as guards. She had them serve her. She had them pull her **chariot**. A chariot is a cart. It has two wheels.

Demeter had a lotus staff and a cornucopia.

Demeter's dragons helped bring food to mankind.

Demeter gave her chariot and dragons to Triptolemus. She had Triptolemus travel the world. She wanted him to teach others how to farm.

Cychreides was a dragon. It had a bad temper. It attacked Salamis. Salamis is an island. A hero kicked Cychreides out. Cychreides fled to Demeter. Demeter kept Cychreides.

Cross-Cultural Connection

Abuk is an African goddess. She's honored by the Dinka people. The Dinka people live in southern Sudan and Ethiopia. Abuk is the goddess of women, water, and gardens. Her symbols are snakes, the moon, and sheep. She's the mother of the god of rain and fertility. She's married to Garang. A rope linked Earth and the heavens. The supreme god, Nhialic, lived in the heavens. Abuk and Garang were the first man and woman on Earth. Nhialic gave Abuk only one grain a day. Abuk and Garang were starving. Abuk disobeyed Nhialic. She planted several grains. She used a hoe. She accidentally hit Nhialic. This made Nhialic angry. He cut the rope. He refused to help them anymore. Since then, Abuk has been responsible for growing things. Abuk saved the world.

CHAPTER 5

A MOTHER'S LOVE

How did Demeter create seasons?

There are many myths about Demeter. The most famous is how she created seasons.

Hades wanted a wife. So, he kidnapped Persephone. Demeter didn't know what happened to her daughter. She searched for Persephone. She traveled far. She searched for nine days and nights. She didn't eat. She didn't drink. She didn't bathe. She didn't rest.

Demeter found out what Hades did. This made her mad. She didn't want Hades to marry Persephone. She didn't want her daughter to live underground forever.

Demeter refused to return to Mount Olympus. She pretended to be mortal. She roamed the earth. She forbade things to grow. She destroyed lands. She destroyed crops. She dried up the earth. This would kill all mortals. The gods needed mortals to worship them.

Demeter and Persephone were goddesses who made things grow.

So, Zeus had to step in. He sent Hermes to the underworld. Hermes was the gods' messenger. He asked Hades to release Persephone. Hades agreed. But he tricked Persephone.

Explained By Science

We now know that it isn't Demeter and Persephone who cause the seasons. Earth spins. This makes night and day. Earth orbits around the sun. This makes a year. A year has four seasons: spring, summer, fall, and winter. Seasons impact what happens on Earth. They're caused by Earth's changing relationship to the sun. As Earth travels around the sun, the amount of sunlight changes for each place on Earth. Earth is tilted. For half of the year, the North Pole has more sun. This means summer. The South Pole has less sun. This is winter. Then, it switches for the other half of the year. Earth's tilt also affects the length of daylight. Summer days have more sunlight. The days are long. This means more energy. More energy means more crops.

Demeter rejected the gods when she lost her daughter.

Persephone had been too sad to eat. But when she learned she was going home, she became happy. She ate Hades's pomegranate seeds. This meant she had to return to Hades. Anyone who tasted the food of Hades had to remain in the underworld.

Persephone had to live with Hades for part of the year. Spring was when Persephone was with Demeter. Winter was when she was with Hades.

Demeter restored Earth's growth during spring. But she became sad when Persephone went to Hades. So, she made Earth cold. She made it **barren**. Barren means not able to grow. She created winter.

Don't anger the goddesses. Demeter had great powers. And she knew how to use them.

 When Persephone came back to Demeter, the earth bloomed.

DID YOU KNOW?

- Demeter's brothers divided the world into three parts. Zeus was god of the sky. Poseidon was god of the seas. Hades was god of the underworld.

- Demeter is also called "She of the Grain," "Giver of Food," and "Law-Bringer."

- Some people think Demeter protected Eleusis. Eleusis is a village. It's near Athens. The city helped her when she was searching for Persephone. The city gave her food and shelter.

- Thesmophoria was a festival. It honored Demeter. It honored fertility. Only women could attend.

- Ancient Romans worshipped gods. Ceres was the Roman version of Demeter. "Cereal" comes from Ceres.

- Ancient Greeks dedicated sneezes to Demeter.

- Sometimes, Demeter appeared as a woman with a black horse's head. She had a black mane. The mane was snakes.

- Demeter was most like her grandmother. Her grandmother was Gaia. Gaia was the supreme mother. She created and gave birth to the universe, earth, and gods.

- Demeter's son Philomelus invented the plow. This made Demeter happy. She turned him into a constellation.

CONSIDER THIS!

TAKE A POSITION Read the 45th Parallel Press book about Hera. How were Hera and Demeter alike? How were they different? Which goddess do you think was more powerful? Argue your point with reasons and evidence.

SAY WHAT? Gods and goddesses did both good and evil things. Explain how Demeter could be good. Explain how she could be evil.

THINK ABOUT IT! Demeter's story helped the ancient Greeks explain the seasons. Create your own myth. Write a story explaining why and how we have four seasons.

LEARN MORE

Fontes, Justine, and Ron Fontes. *Demeter and Persephone: Spring Held Hostage*. Minneapolis: Graphic Universe, 2007.

Lupton, Hugh, Daniel Morden, and Carole Henaff (illustrator). *Demeter and Persephone*. Cambridge: Barefoot Books, 2013.

GLOSSARY

barren (BAR-uhn) not fertile, not able to grow

chariot (CHAR-ee-uht) two-wheeled cart pulled by animals

constellation (kahn-stuh-LAY-shuhn) star pattern

cornucopia (kor-nuh-KOH-pee-uh) container that looks like a goat's horn

fertility (fur-TIL-ih-tee) capable of growing a lot

immortal (ih-MOR-tuhl) living forever

maidens (MAY-duhnz) beautiful young women

mortal (MOR-tuhl) human

Olympians (uh-LIM-pee-uhnz) rulers of the gods who lived on Mount Olympus

sheaves (SHEEVZ) bundles

siblings (SIB-lingz) brothers and sisters

Sirens (SYE-ruhnz) women turned into monsters

Titans (TYE-tunz) giant gods who ruled before the Olympians

INDEX